DOGS

MUTTS

STUART A. KALLEN

ABDO & Daughters

Published by Abdo & Daughters, 4940 Viking Drive, Suite 622, Edina, Minnesota 55435.

Library bound edition distributed by Rockbottom Books, Pentagon Tower, P.O. Box 36036, Minneapolis, Minnesota 55435.

Printed in the United States.

Cover Photo credit: Peter Arnold, Inc.

Interior Photo credits: Peter Arnold, Inc.

Edited by Rosemary Wallner

Library of Congress Cataloging-in-Publication Data

Kallen, Stuart A., 1955
      Mutt / Stuart A. Kallen.
   p. cm. — (Dogs)
Includes bibliographical references (p.24) and index.
  ISBN 1-56239-450-9
1. Dogs—Juvenile literature. [1. Dogs.] I. Title. II. Series: Kallen, Stuart A., 1955-
Dogs.
SF426.5.K35   1995
636.7—dc20   95-928
                                    CIP
                                    AC

ABOUT THE AUTHOR
Stuart Kallen has written over 80 children's books, including many environmental science books.

CONTENTS

DOGS AND WOLVES: CLOSE COUSINS

Dogs have been living with humans for more than 12,000 years. Today, hundreds of millions of dogs live in the world. Over 400 **breeds** exist.

All dogs are related to the wolf. Some dogs—like tiny poodles or Great Danes—may look nothing like the wolf. But under their skin, every dog shares many feelings and **traits** with the wolf.

All dogs are related to the wolf. This is a gray wolf in a northern Montana forest.

MUTTS

In the beginning, all dogs were mutts—**crossbreeds**. Then people began **breeding** dogs for certain **traits**—like hunting and guarding. Today, there are over 400 types of **purebred** dogs in the world. But most dogs are still crossbreed mutts.

In the beginning, all dogs were mutts.

WHAT THEY'RE LIKE

There are hundreds of types of dogs to choose from, but many people think mutts make the best pets. Mutts are often stronger, better-tempered, and healthier than **purebreds**. Some people also think mutts are smarter than purebred dogs.

Because of this, most circus and performing dogs are mutts.

Mutts are often stronger, smarter, and healthier than purebreds.

COAT AND COLOR

Mutts come in dozens of colors: white, tan, brown, black, and colors in-between.

Mutts can have a wavy **coat** or straight coat. Some have no coat at all! They may be almost bald, like a Chihuahua. Or they may have long hair like an English sheepdog.

Mutts can have wavy hair or straight hair. They also come in dozens of colors.

SIZE

The smallest mutts may be tiny, like a Pekinese. The biggest mutts may be huge, like a Great Dane. As with humans, there is an average size for mutts. A middle-sized mutt will weigh 20 to 40 pounds (9 to 18 kg) and stand 12 to 24 inches (30 to 61 cm) from the ground to its shoulders.

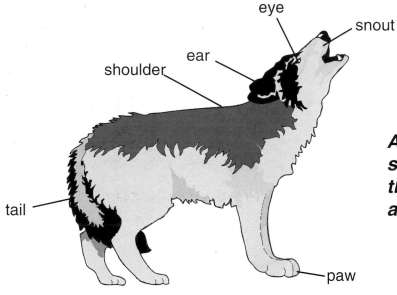

eye

snout

ear

shoulder

tail

paw

All dogs share the same features with their common ancestor, the wolf.

A middle-sized mutt will weigh 20 to 40 pounds (9 to 18 kg).

CARE

Dogs need the same things as humans: a warm bed, food, water, exercise, and lots of love.

Many mutts have hair that needs to be brushed every day. If the dog is not **groomed**, its **coat** will become matted and tangled. Sometimes, the dog will need a bath and its nails clipped.

All dogs need shots every year. These shots stop diseases such as **distemper** and **hepatitis**.

As a member of your household, your dog expects love and attention. Dogs enjoy human contact and like to **retrieve** sticks or catch Frisbees.

Mutts enjoy human contact and like to retrieve sticks or catch Frisbees.

FEEDING

All dogs like meat. But they also need a well-balanced **diet**. Most dog foods—dry or canned—will give the mutt proper **nutrition**.

When you buy a puppy, find out what it has been eating and continue that diet. A small puppy needs four to five small meals a day. By six months of age, it will need only two meals a day. By one year, a single evening feeding will be enough.

Dogs must be exercised every day so they don't gain weight. Walking, running, and playing together will keep you and your dog happy and healthy. Give your dog a hard rubber ball with which to play.

Dogs need a lot of fresh water. Keep a full dish of water next to the dog's food bowl and change it daily.

Mutts must be exercised every day so they don't gain weight.

THINGS THEY NEED

Dogs need a quiet place to sleep. A soft dog bed in a quiet corner is the best place for a mutt to sleep. Most dogs need to live indoors. If the dog must live outside, give it a dry, **insulated** dog house.

Mutts love to run. A fenced-in yard is the perfect home for a dog. If that is not possible, use a chain on a runner.

In most cities and towns, a dog must be leashed when going for a walk.

Dogs also need a license. Dog licenses have the owner's name, address, and telephone number on them. If the dog runs away, the owners can be called.

In most cities and towns, a dog must be leashed when going for a walk.

PUPPIES

Average mutts can have three to six puppies. The dog is **pregnant** for about nine weeks. When she is ready to give birth, she needs a dark place away from noises. If your dog is pregnant, give her a strong box lined with an old blanket. She will have her puppies there.

Puppies are tiny and helpless when born. They arrive about half-an-hour apart. The mother licks them clean which helps them start breathing. Their eyes are shut, making them blind for their first nine days. They are also deaf for about ten days.

Dogs are **mammals**. They drink milk from their mother.

After about four weeks, puppies will grow teeth. At this time, separate them from their mother and give the puppies soft dog food.

Mutt puppies at play as the mother looks on.

GLOSSARY

BREED - A group of animals with the same traits; also, to produce young.

COAT - The dog's outer covering (hair).

CROSSBREED - To breed with different kinds of dogs; also, mutt.

DIET - The usual kind of food and drink.

DISTEMPER (dis-TEMP-pur) - A disease of dogs and certain other animals, caused by a virus.

GROOM - To brush and take care of an animal.

HEPATITIS (hep-uh-TIE-tis) - The swelling of the liver caused by a virus.

INSULATION (in-sue-LAY-shun) - Something that stops heat loss.

MAMMAL - A class of animals, including humans, that have hair and feed their young milk.

NUTRITION (new-TRISH-un) - Food; nourishment.

PREGNANT - With one or more babies growing inside the body.

PUREBRED - Bred from the same kinds of dogs.

RETRIEVE - To return or bring back.

SPECIES (SPEE-seas) - A group of related plants or animals.

TRAIT - A feature or characteristic.

VETERINARIAN (vet-ur-ih-NAIR-ee-un)- A doctor trained to take care of animals.

Index

BIBLIOGRAPHY

American Kennel Club. *The Complete Dog Book*. New York: Macmillan, 1992.

Clutton-Brock, Juliet. *Dog*. New York: Alfred A. Knopf, 1991.

The Complete Book of the Dog. New York: Holt, Rinehart, & Winston, 1985.

Frye, Fredric L. *Mutts*. Hauppauge, New York: Barron's Educational Series, Inc.: 1989

Sylvester, Patricia. *The Reader's Digest Illustrated Book of Dogs*. New York: The Reader's Digest Association, 1984.